PRIVATE PLEASURES

Connie Bensley was born in south-west London, and has always lived there, apart from wartime evacuation. Until her retirement she worked as a secretary to doctors and to an MP and as a medical copywriter.

She has published four books with Bloodaxe: *Central Reservations: New & Selected Poems* (1990), which draws on two earlier collections, *Progress Report* and *Moving In*; and more recently, *Choosing To Be a Swan* (1994), *The Back & the Front of It* (2000) and *Private Pleasures* (2007).

PRIVATE PLEASURES

Connie Bensley

BLOODAXE BOOKS

ISBN: 978 1 85224 756 0

First published 2007 by
Bloodaxe Books Ltd,
Highgreen,
Tarset,
Northumberland NE48 1RP.

www.bloodaxebooks.com
For further information about Bloodaxe titles
please visit our website or write to
the above address for a catalogue.

Bloodaxe Books Ltd acknowledges
the financial assistance of
Arts Council England, North East.

Cover design: Neil Astley & Pamela Robertson-Pearce.

Cover printing: J. Thomson Colour Printers Ltd, Glasgow.

Printed in Great Britain by
Bell & Bain Limited, Glasgow, Scotland.

For my friends

ACKNOWLEDGEMENTS

Acknowledgements are due to the editors of the following publications, in which some of these poems first appeared: *Acumen, The London Magazine, Mslexia, North, Orbis, The Reader, Seam, Smiths Knoll, Stand* and *The Times Literary Supplement.*

'In a Flash' and 'Funeral Dog' were broadcast on *The Verb* (BBC Radio 3).

CONTENTS

Under Your Skin

You may take it out on a lead;
you may give birth to it
you may be its child.

You will know which one it is
and it knows you.
It knows its power.

If it turns its back on you once
you say goodbye to sleep
all the live-long night.

Awakening

After a pint or two of Shires
the gas man is asleep in his van
on the common. The sun is hot on his face,
his feet are on the dashboard.

He dreams himself into a garden
with that lovely girl who does the weather
in figure-hugging turquoise...but his wife
is tip-tapping down the garden path towards them.

The tapping gets into his ear, like an earwig,
and he opens his eyes to a blurred face
outside the glass. It is Mrs Boiler-Problem
of Fifteen Park Drive.

Flakes of ash are clinging to her hair
and in the sooty darkness of her face, her eyes
are red and mad. She is mouthing words
no decent man wants to hear from a woman.

All the Kissing We Do Now

Not just the greeting and parting kisses,
but the maybe-this-person-could-give-me-a-contract
kiss; the what-was-her-name? kiss
the kiss electric, behind the coat rack.

The invasive kiss. The viral kiss.
The kiss that spreads something like wildfire
and keeps you awake half the night
for more reasons than you can shake a stick at.

Biography

When you were cut open,
the small bones of your lovers
were discovered inside you.
Shrunken skulls, tiny ankle bones,
femurs in miniature.

We arranged your prey with tweezers,
recognising a tooth here,
a digit there. What a big beast you were!
You could swallow a chorus line;
a sixth form; a pew-full of worshippers.

Now we are fighting over you,
stabbing each other with our spiky pens.
We want to eat you up.
It will make us famously potent.

Colouring Book

Here is the Common where she used to play.
Here are the trees she climbed and here is the path
twisted and shady.

There is the clover underneath her feet,
colour it pink. There are her new blue sandals,
see how they run.

Here is a stranger, following down the path
and into a glade. Did they meet in the glade?
Turn over the page.

Now they are out of sight. Is that a bird
or a cry that we hear? See how the sparrows
fly from the bush.

End Game

Those interminable games of chess...
I think it's the only reason he comes to see me.

    Those interminable games of chess.
    She always has the board out, waiting.

Generally I let him win. After all, he's come
from Chislehurst. It seems sad
to come so far for nothing
but tea and cake.

    Sometimes I try to let her win,
    but she's not much of a player.
    At least she makes a decent pot
    of Orange Pekoe.

I could be having a siesta
or catching up with my patchwork.
But that's just selfishness.

    If I made an excuse next week,
    I could get back to my notes on the Crimea.
    But she'd miss me so much.

De-familiarisation

Now that his memory has gone,
his house is a treasure trove:
each drawer a surprise, each cupboard
a revelation.

Discovery is his obsession,
the ranks of photographs (a wife? a daughter?)
are his clues, studied at night,
unfamiliar by morning.

Daily he takes his walk
round the square. He knows his home
by its fig tree.

The house takes him back in, reveals its contents
to his astonished eye.

First Names...

...as used by almost everyone –
matey electricians, nurses, and so on –
are certainly egalitarian.
But something is lost –
that breachable formality of the surname
like close-fitting gloves or bound-up hair.

Once it was 'Miss Jones'.
Across a polished desk.
The surname and the desk
being obstacles to congress
as formidable as a bolster in a bed,
that is to say – slight but piquant.

Certainties

She knew he was attracted to her
because of the way he avoided meeting her eye;
because of the shy way he failed
to take the chair next to hers,
and because – to get closer to her –
he pretended to flirt with her sister.

After he left the party
he was still too diffident to phone,
or even to write.

Someone had taken photographs.
He was in one of them,
turned away and out of focus,
but she kept it. Year after year
it grew more potent.

Heartfelt

My broken heart, just out of plaster,
Beats in a half-hearted way.

You could make it beat much faster
You could nurse it through the day.

Save my heart from more disaster
Love's a skill I've yet to master
But my need for you is vaster
Than an uncut Passion Play.

Under the Shawl

Parting from you in Moscow
hurt like frostbite. You in your
unfamiliar hat, me in my purple shawl.

Round Red Square once more, arms linked,
eyes locked, then off to the airport,
that crepuscular cavern.

I waved you off. Belarus – such a good name,
like a Roman Emperor or his horse.
What is keeping you there?

I hear that girls in Belarus
play fast and loose: cover your ears
against their siren call

and make your way back
to Moscow. Here, I will take you, I promise,
under my purple shawl.

Sibling

On his sixtieth birthday it happened at last.
Dear Ricardo, his mother's note read:
I shall come out of hospital on the 14th,
and hope you can stay with me for a few days,
until I'm on my feet again.

No mention of Hermione! No mention
of his spoilt, domineering sister!
Whistling to himself, he unearthed his three
presentable shirts and folded them neatly
into a clean Tesco bag.

Out of My Mouth

I've heard all my opinions before
and I am tired of them.
They fall heavily out of my mouth
and lie around
like tiny, wizened children.

I don't blame you
for stamping on them.
We will do it together
and when the massacre is over
I will begin again –

my thoughts darting and colourful
as tropical birds.
You will hardly know me.
I'll hardly know myself.
So that's a start, anyway.

Background

When they met a second time
he persuaded her to come and see his garden –
which he'd mentioned on their first date.

The scene was one of chaos:
great scoops of earth flung about;
dank water in the depressions,

the whole edged by dark greenery
(Cypress, Leylandii, something spindly,
underplanted with Bugleweed).

In the centre, a small upright shed
crammed with planks of wood and tubing.
A foreground of buckets, lumps of stone,

something large and rusty. Mud.
He explained his plan: underground streams,
and a grotto half hidden by spotted laurels.

When will it be finished? she asked.
This (he calculated) *is year three,*
but of course a garden is never quite finished.

The soft wet ground sucked at her stilettoes
so despite herself
she had to grab hold of him.

Deadheading

The telephone
is easily subdued.
I use a pillow
and a dark cloth.

That is reasonable.

But I don't like the way
I keep curling up
in a foetal position;
or wrapping myself
in the curtain
when someone knocks.

That's not the way I was brought up
in those rainbow days
of cake forks
drawn threadwork
and that never-ending task
of deadheading.

Open Plan

As usual, the escalator is a temptation.
Riding up from Handbags to Furniture
she peers down at China and Glass –
a department full of white lights
and winking facets, of delicately poised
tea services, of crystal jugs and bowls,
all inviting her (*come on, come on*)
to plunge head first over the rail.
What a satisfying smash it would make,
and how it would divert the sales assistants
for weeks:...*she looked quite ordinary*
...half the Waterford and Crown Derby gone...
Tessa from Scarves tried a tourniquet
...the ambulance was quick, but not quick enough.

Now she has finished in Furniture. Perhaps
she should go down by the back stairs?
But the escalator cannot be resisted.
Overtly calm, heart racing,
(a novice diver to a high board)
she steps towards it.

Needs

I need to go shopping for mascara. He needs
to get to the pub before closing time.

You need to get out more
and put the past behind you.

She needs somewhere to sleep.
A lean-to would do for the night.

They need a square meal, or at least
a handful of maize.

She needs water. A cupful
could save her.

Date

They waited an age to be seated.
The head waiter loomed, receded, made specious
promises. But in the end they fell asleep
standing up in the bar, like beasts in a field.

Finally they gave up; stumbled home to forage
in her fridge. That bottle of stir-through sauce
with nothing to stir it through.
Those weary biscuits. That apple.

Their sleep was disturbed by the pluck
of the wind at the blind,
and his nightmare about the waiters
killing and eating his parrot.

Lesson

Painfully soon after his birthday
she came across the scarf she had knitted for him.
It was in the Oxfam shop,
flung over a bargain rail.

The soft wool came back to her hand;
she remembered the careful joins between the grey
and the indigo; the final pressing, and –
my God what a fool – the folding in silver tissue.

The rebuttal of love, she thought,
has its obligations, its necessary courtesies.
Buying back the scarf, twisting it round her wrist,
she planned to meet him one more time.

Advice

– so kindly meant,
so freely given –
so very often wrong.

A Change in the Weather

This is the rough you're given with the smooth.
This is the bad hand after all those aces.

This is the nerve that's jumping in your tooth:
This is the cold look after the embraces.

This is the something nasty in the sink.
This is the tentacle that grips you tightly.

This is the thought you cannot bear to think.
This is the way you think it, daily, nightly.

Long-term Residents Welcome

When they met, breathless, in the foyer
the wheelchairs might have alerted them
but they were distracted.

How they slammed the door of their room and sprung
into bed like swimmers into water. How many
lengths and widths, how many different strokes,

until, beached and comatose,
they were shaken awake
by the ambulance bell below;

then they remembered the handrails, the stairlift,
the half-glimpsed crutches
in the hall stand.

Somehow they couldn't laugh it off.
It was too near the knuckle
of the real world.

The message calling her home was an invention:
but his expression of relief
was nakedly genuine.

Loose Connections

It's hard to capture it on paper,
this elusive shape-shifting idea.
Yet if he can crystallise it,
hone it, make it succinct,

it could be his memorial –
a tiny atom of philosophy
handed down to posterity.
At any rate a footnote

to some greater work.
He takes his fountain pen
and a pad of lined paper,
and after seventeen minutes

(absently watching a magpie
trawling the roof gutter opposite)
he finds that he has written:
    Fix MOT. And find out
    how you get divorced.

Landscape with Figure

I can't reclaim the landscape of my mind.
Whichever way I turn, I see you there.
Friends say: 'A change of scene will help.' I find
that when the scene is changed, you reappear.

The figure in the distance on the beach,
her brown hair blowing, pointing out to sea –
however fast I run, she's out of reach
and when I call, she never turns to me.

I went back to our park. Remember how
we picnicked by the lake, and in the rain
we sheltered in the folly? Even now
I see you down each vista.
                              I'm in pain
The beauty of each landscape mocks my lack.
The sun shines cheerlessly. You won't come back.

Extinction

In the Pleistocene of their relationship
he learned to talk
and she learned to walk upright.
A pity, then, that they are struck
by this Ice Age

Alibi

They climbed into bed as usual,
the duvet sighing down over them

and after she turned out the lamp
she saw her arm in its white sleeve

still faintly stretched towards the light
like an interesting ghost

though actually it was back in bed
taking no part in the proceedings.

Recycling

The word-lorry is coming,
swallowing up last week's news,
spiriting away yesterday's SPECIAL OFFERS.

She throws in the bundle of his letters
then changes her mind and runs down the lane
in pursuit. Too late.

His words have gone: lost their grip,
lost their charge of pleasure and pain.
They're buried under an avalanche

of headlines, crosswords, obits –
racing towards oblivion,
stiffening to papier-mâché in the rain.

Marrying the Car

He loved his car above everything,
polishing, cherishing – always
easing into it with a serious smile.
Giving it quality time.

Partners came and went. Hormones raged
in his blood, then unaccountably
drained away. Annoyingly
his last wife left with all his classical CDs.

Is it wrong to love a car?
Who can say. Some people love a house,
a song, a dog, a view.
Whatever helps you through the day will do.

Vacillation

Steering my dirigible
over the souks of Istanbul
my thoughts are mocking birds,
fugitive as this moonlight
on broken water.

I imagine you down below
perhaps in the mosque,
your golden slippers neatly paired,
your bowed head gleaming
in that tile-reflected light.

Think of me threading the sky
wondering whether to fly away,
or come back to earth –
the doubtful moon looking first
over my left shoulder, then over my right.

Street Theatre

Where I live, it never gets dark.
At any time of night you can climb
out of bed and see from your window
the houses crammed shoulder to shoulder
and lit like a stage set, bright and golden.
It must cost the council a fortune.
The cars glisten, the street is absolutely ready
for something to happen, for something to enter
stage left, though usually nothing does –
just a fox, perhaps, molesting a rubbish sack.
Or you might spot another insomniac at his window
waving briefly, turning back to his bed
for a last attempt at sleep, penning those sheep
in the fold, hoping for a spell of oblivion
before the cold shock of six o'clock.

The Big Question

Quiet as murmuring pigeons,
the builders are talking to each other
and stabbing the floorboards with a screwdriver:
Look, Rick, the wood's all gone.

Caught it just in time, Pete.
We're looking at new timber joists –
and that concrete's got to go for starters.

They sit back on their haunches
and eye each other reflectively,
like doctors making a tricky diagnosis.

The householder shifts from foot to foot,
waiting to ask his big question.

Private Pleasures

Up to my elbows
in the juice
of a huge, ripe,
perfumed, unmanageable
mango,
I suddenly wonder
if I am being
watched.

Mango-moustached,
I hastily pull down
the blind.

Some things
are best enjoyed
in privacy.

A Question of Taste

I linger near *Tabouleh* and *Spiralli*
thinking sun, sea, ruins.

A grey-haired man leans forward
pondering names which sound like
old battles or obscure dynasties:
Sambousec, *Keftedes*, *Souvlakia*, *Feta*.

Pushing the spectacles up his nose
he presses on to the Anglo-Saxon section
where his eye falls, with fond recognition,
on *Toad in the Hole*.

Nasturtiums

*On 10 August 2003 the temperature in London
exceeded a hundred degrees for the first time*

Hotter than Singapore. Or Mississippi.
Or that time in Assisi.

Only the nasturtiums are vigorous.
Their fleshy stems shoot out fast as snakes
towards the door: their red tongues
rasp the paintwork.

In the morning they'll have colonised
the house, thrusting through open windows,
winding round the lamps, the toaster,
the banisters, the leg of our bed.

The House Opposite

Her bedroom curtains, on this hot night,
are not completely closed,
so that he occasionally glimpses
a tranche of thigh, a fall of lace,

and – several times – her left knee.
He tries to remember
the literary term
for the part representing the whole.

When he passes her in the street
he smiles politely, glancing
towards her left knee, with which
he is so much more familiar than she imagines.

Waving

Gazing from my bedroom window, admiring
the sun on the marigolds, I suddenly see
a woman at her own window opposite.
She is waving and waving.

I pull myself together. Is this an emergency?
Perhaps there is a burglar in the house,
or perhaps her husband has collapsed
against the bedroom door.

I wave back vigorously and reach for my binoculars.
And she is not waving at all, but cleaning her windows.
Her white cloth soars and plunges. Fortunately
she has not noticed me.

Dove

Today, the visiting white dove
at last took seed from my hand,
his pecking a considered blend
of delicacy and preference
his beak ridiculously pink.

His crimson eye, gold-rimmed,
gleamed up at me and his breast,
soft as a pillow against my fingertips,
vibrated with faint croonings.

Leda's affaire flew into my mind
and out again.

Brief Encounter with a Horse Whisperer

Tonight, on sofas all over the country,
women are watching through a veil
of tears, as the credits roll
and the wife drives back to her husband –
leaving behind Robert Redford,
who is radiating craggy sadness
on a horse. On a hill.

A thousand women, in synchronous dreams,
do their level best to comfort him.

Song

When I walked back from your house last week
it seemed so mild for October.
The last of the light was gold
over the river, and when I passed the pond
five geese flew up in formation
banking low over the rooftops. Babies
were being wheeled home. The late flowers
in the front gardens were curiously brilliant –
the yellow evening primrose, blue love-in-a-mist;
a shower of white solanum, shimmering.
I was singing, under my breath,
the song we practised together
but I don't think anyone noticed.

The Case of the Distracted Postman

The postman is in love
and all of us are bearing the brunt.

My newsletter from the Secular Society
went to the Vicar. The Vicar's bank statement

arrived at Number 33, who steamed it open
then put something extra in the collection

on Sunday. Coarse seaside postcards
have caused offence to Lavinia, who was

in mourning, and I personally was expecting
a love letter, rather than

the Bus Timetable, copies of which
I keep receiving, day after day.

We are getting together to offer him
counselling. Every day he is seen

staring into the pond, his disordered letter-sack
trembling on the brink.

Lovers in the London Aquarium

In this low light, they hardly need
to be discreet. Their embraces shimmer back
at them from glass, from glaucous eyes.

Mock alarm at the sharks
drives them even closer together
though you'd hardly think it possible.

They are hypnotised by the eels,
slipping in and out of their rock crevices.
Now she nestles inside his jacket.

In the mangrove swamp, roots
intertwine. It is hot and dark.
They could linger there all day.

But a more prosaic hunger drives them, blinking,
into the daylight, where the wind
off the steely river is whipping up a cold shower.

Piccadilly in the Sunshine

The roadsweeping machine
is wheezing along past the commissionaires
in their Russian-prince uniforms

and its brushy little wheels buzz a path
through the polyglot strollers
with their bulging bags from Fortnum's;

and it weaves between the dark-suited men,
who are on their mobiles cutting serious deals
with Chicago or China or Chile,

though surely they should be saying

    Mother, it's such a lovely day
    why not ditch the Bridge
    and come and have tea at the Ritz?
    ...yes, profiteroles...
    and then we'll find some deck chairs;
    the park is so green and tempting today.

Dora

Serene, chaste, not much of a thinker,
Dora always stood by the pier glass
in our mother's bedroom,
headlessly reflected
and ready to play her impassive role.

Sometimes she blossomed
into rosy gauze
or sea-green taffeta;
but these frivolities
never quite suited her.

Mother pinned, stitched, fitted
and then subdued billowing
rainbow flounces into cardboard boxes,
sending them off to flirt
round hot unknown ballrooms.

But Dora kept her nun-like reserve
even when you pulled her clothes off,
even when you stuck pins in her.
Her single leg was polished and sturdy.
No foxtrots for you, Dora, we told her.

Then

That was the year, if you remember,
when the Last Request Bill was introduced.
Anyone over seventy was eligible.

The colours of the cubicles
were rich as Egypt; the couches
deeply sprung, the automatic sleep plungers
smooth and silent.

Some critics objected at first, do you recall?
But soon the self-propelled wheelchairs
were rolling up across the bumpy pavement –
later to be left outside,
empty but garlanded.

Universal Primer

When you set out to repaint a room,
those old diaries must be moved from the shelf.

First blow off the dust, then –
because you have them in your hand –

look up what you were doing this time
last year, and ten years ago,

and twenty. You'll probably need
a coffee, because of the dust

and to help you remember who it was
you were in love with – referred to

by those guarded initials – in 1978.
A newspaper cutting flies out

about a gynaecologist – and then one
heavily marked, about a window-cleaner:

surely neither was the mystery man, and yet...
some memory falteringly stirs. You read on

until dusk, then reach for the light switch.
A still life is sharply revealed

of sugar soap, white spirit and universal primer.

To Those People I've Annoyed by My Infatuations

First there was the boy with the hamster
who blushed and became monosyllabic;

then there was the music master
who ignored my notes;

was it the gynaecologist next?
Such men cultivate deafness;

and what about the psephologist?
My predilections were strange in those days.

Finally, that Austrian with no chin and a bow tie
who moved out of the district.

I'd like to apologise to you all
for the inconvenience caused

by my tears and sighs,
intrusions and lingering looks.

I am quite better now.

Page-turner

My father and mother were honest, though poor.
'Skip all that!' cried the Bellman in haste.
LEWIS CARROLL,
'The Hunting of the Snark'

Yes, get straight on to the mystery woman
acrobat; or at any rate

the disgraceful Rites of Passage carry-ons.
Spare us the years of tranquillity

and for God's sake don't rabbit on
about how he reclaimed his garden season by season;

or that book on Baudelaire he kept failing to write.
We'd better examine the stormy marriages,

the break-outs from the rehab centre,
and most particularly, the rumours of incest.

Any serious student of psychology
needs to know about the incest.

Register his sad decline and don't skip the death –
though we'll certainly flinch at the pain and indignity.

The scenes at the funeral between
the mistresses makes a wry postscript –

and there we are: a life begun and ended
in a few hours, with hardly a hint of boredom.

Pack

No ducking stool,
no thumbscrew:

the hangman comes disguised
as a bloke –

with a camera
a million short words

and a heavy boot.
The victim survives long enough

for some sport.

The Speech

The voice goes on, a flat, unending drone.
When did he start? Today or yesterday?
Ring, ring, please ring, I urge my mobile phone.

The audience has aged and turned to stone.
A few slip out ('I'm off to the café').
The voice goes on, a flat, unending drone.

A pause. Our hopes are raised! But then a groan –
He carries on. I close my eyes and pray:
Ring, ring, please ring, I urge my mobile phone.

A woman faints: they dab her with Cologne.
She's better off unconscious I should say.
The voice goes on, a flat unending drone.

Why can't I leave? I've no will of my own.
Some astral force decrees that I must stay.
Ring, ring, please ring, I beg my mobile phone.
The voice goes on, a flat, unending drone.

Best Before

What preoccupied you, in your final illness,
was your fridge. We had to promise you

as a matter of urgency, to check the dates
on the eggs, to be ruthless with the milk;

to bin the archaeological mysteries
at the back of the shelves.

We jettisoned whiskery cheese, fluorescent bacon,
an egg yolk stiffening in a tiny pot.

The moment this ritual cleansing was complete
your breathing eased and you slept,

waking just the once, when you tried a final joke –
something to do with a dustman and an undertaker.

Funeral Dog

Having a dog at your funeral
made all the difference.

The dog was quiet, snuff-coloured
and nondescript. We edged round
awkwardness by asking each other
his name, or bending over him
for a private moment of grief.

He seemed to know that this was his work
for the day. Afterwards, the rewards –
a wild run on the common, a biscuit
from the tin with the hollyhocks,
then the long stretched-out oblivion
of a job well done.

We Are So Many

In the bus, next to my knee, is a huge leg,
pale and bristly. It is part of a big man
in tiny shorts – a weight-lifter, perhaps
or someone from a genetically bulky family.

It sets me thinking about the problems of dissolution.
Can the crematoria cope with such solidity?
Otherwise, it's up to the earth to swallow us,
bus-fulls, train-loads, arenas of us –

and so much of the earth out of action
under patios and shopping malls.
At my gaze, the man shifts his leg uneasily,
and rings the bell. The doors hiss open for him.

Those Old Gods

They were always interfering – blowing over
ships, turning people into trees
on the merest whim.

The new generation are still at it:
setting off volcanoes, summoning
earthquakes, spreading plagues.

But something is missing.
It might be the knack of impersonation
or malicious playfulness.

Occasionally you catch an echo
of their old style: someone half-man, half-frog
trips you up on the bus,

or, in the half-light of dawn,
you catch your topiary bird
creeping back into its hedge

and settling impassively
on its root, the earth at its foot
barely disturbed.

Horticulture

Something in the compost bin
keeps trying to grow; raising
skinny white arms in pathetic supplication.

I turn the heap, crush and bury it,
but repeatedly it climbs up again,
refusing to rot.

Is there a metaphorical message in this –
am I meant to infer some truth
about Hope, Endurance and Rebirth?

Finally I give in, lift it out
and carefully plant it in the damp earth.
At once it keels over, staging a dramatic death.

In a Flash

You hand me a photograph, and in it,
your chin, with its five o'clock shadow
is a foil to the tender cheek
of your first-born.

But wait, it is only a moment since
you were the baby, lying on my bed,
staring curiously sideways,
as if getting to know the wallpaper,
or working out some plan.

You'll notice how quickly it all happens.
The photos fly in and out of the albums
like snow, like melting snow.

Single Room

The hotel sheets, though crisp and white,
vestigially hold the scent
of someone else's life:

someone else whose fleeting essence
shares my bed; someone whose presence
starts a train of reminiscence.

Cinnamon? Or aftershave?
Like a name you can't remember,
half-forgotten, half-familiar.

Why Didn't You Tell Me You Were Dead?

It was odd the way I found out:
coming across your name
on a plaque on that bench
(in Roman caps, HE LOVED THIS VIEW).

I thought of you –
never one to commend any view –
rebellious, cranky, funny;
touching my life then losing touch.

The years wound back
to you, leaning forward
either to kiss or to mock:
your beard vibrant with intent.

Not a bad idea, these markers
we invent, stretching our time
that single heartbeat more,
cairns, gravestones, pyramids,
plaques, words written
on a dark and shifting floor.

Artefact

This poem will
disintegrate
as you read it –
see the words
fade
and fall apart,
see the curator
sweep them
into the
corner
with his
dusty
broom –
lock
the glass case,
turn,
and leave
the room.